Damaged Goods

Hurt By the Church

Elder Treneé L. Pruitt

Foreword by:
Overseer Jonathan J.H. McReynolds

DAMAGED GOODS
Hurt By the Church
Copyright © 2014
Treneé L. Pruitt

All scripture references are from the Authorized King James Version of the Bible, unless otherwise marked.

References marked AMP are from the Amplified Bible, © Copyright 1987 by the Zondervan Publishing House.

References from The Message, © Copyright 2002 by NavPress Publishing Group.

References marked NLT are from the New Living Translation, © Copyright 2004 by Tyndale House Publishers, Inc.

References marked New Century are from the New Century Translation, © Copyright 1991 by Word Publishing.

References marked NIV are from the New International Version, © Copyright 1991 by Holman Bible Publishers.

ISBN: 978-0-615-98002-7

DEDICATION

I dedicate this book to:

My parents, Robert and Mary Pruitt, the most wonderful people that God created for me. I am ever so grateful and thankful that God chose them to be my parents. They have shown me how to live and love beyond the damages of life.

My siblings, Julian, Annise, Ruby and Tangeé, I love you all so much.

To **every person** who openly shared their stories and advice for the world, you know who you are.

To **everyone** who has encountered some hurt, difficulties and damages while serving, seeking and giving God glory.

"Wherefore let them that suffer according to the will of God commit the keeping of their souls to him in well doing, as unto a faithful Creator." 1 Peter 4:19

TABLE OF CONTENTS

ACKNOWLEDGMENTS

I would like to thank:

God, the Almighty Creator of all things: It is through your Holy Spirit that this work has been accomplished.

Neesee: Your prayers and being there no matter what was definitely felt.

Annaka: Thanks for staying up with me through the long nights.

Overseer Jonathan J.H. McReynolds: Your support means more than you can ever imagine. I am glad that you are my pastor. Thank you for writing the foreword.

Pastor J. Renee Richardson: Thanks for being my spiritual big sister, mentor and friend.

You, the reader: Thank you for having this book in your hand. I am glad that you chose this book and have an interest in the subject matter. Perhaps, you may be a Damaged Good that experienced hurt by a brother or sister in the church? In fact, every person has been damaged in one way or another. I hope you will allow the information and stories in this book to give you moments of self reflection; as well as, seeing yourself and others through the eyes of God.

Foreword

Elder Pruitt embraces a dynamic task of speaking to an often invisible demographic within the life of the church. Those who are damaged goods within the church. Damaged goods are individuals who possess potential, value and anointing; however, they underachieve within the kingdom because they have been damaged by their church experience. Elder Pruitt apprehends the oxymoronic existence of people living in the status of damaged goods within a spiritual culture that is mandated to reconcile humanity back unto God and repair the damage that sin and the world has inflicted upon their lives.

Elder Pruitt also brings forth a harsh reality of the church culture. That reality is the church often ignores or goes into spiritual denial regarding the existence of damaged goods within the church. The church has often operated with a paradigm and praxis that aborts its responsibility to heal those who are damaged because it attempts to avoid the realities of its own culture and praxis. Thus, Elder Pruitt addresses the systemic problem of damaged goods within the church with a systematic assessment of the church, the damaged, the leadership, the core source of damage and how to heal the damaged. This piece of literature is a powerful tool for the damaged, those who have been the source of damage and those who are facilitating the healing and recovery of the damaged.

Elder Pruitt identifies a critical element regarding damaged goods within the church. The damaging of the Lord's people is not exclusive to acts of insensitivity or malicious intent. The book reveals through the interviews of the damaged that often people are damaged by the systems of the church structure and function as well as people being out of order regarding their role and authority within the body. This is critical because many times within congregational life this means of hurt is more common than the malicious acts of individuals.

Elder Pruitt effectively reconciles this dilemma by

establishing what the church is, who the church is and what our expressed role is within the context of ministering to humanity until the Lord's return. This book gives a refreshing and empowering look at how the body can engage in the sacred and glorious act of healing a broken humanity from within the confines of the church.   Throughout this book, Elder Pruitt provides great hope for those who consider themselves as being damaged goods or recognize they are serving within a ministry context that is populated with damaged goods.

Elder Pruitt is uniquely qualified to address this relevant social and spiritual issue. She has served as an elder in various ministry contexts and has actively engaged those who are damaged goods. Thus, she writes with literary authority on the subject not based solely upon research of the subject matter but living out the subject matter in her life and calling.

Overseer Jonathan J.H. McReynolds
Oakley Full Gospel Baptist Church
Columbus, Ohio

Introduction

When we attend church there are some people among us who are damaged from the various challenges of life. As a matter of fact, we are all damaged in some way or another. Some are more damaged than others and seek to be healed of damage. At least once a week, we gather in our place of worship seeking the presence of God and the manifestation of His promises. However, our focus shifts when the "saint" at the door does not smile or speak. Our focus shifts when the pastor or the leader walks by as if we are invisible. Our focus shifts when the choir is in big disarray. Our focus shifts when there are assigned seats in the congregation. Our focus shifts when it is time to give an offering. Our focus shifts when we become more concerned about a person's fashion apparel. Our focus shifts when the pains of life are beating us to a pulp, and nobody in this place of worship shows compassion. Unfortunately, the focus shifts away from the original purpose of praise, worship, basking in the presence of God, and seeing the manifestation of his promises. Thus, Damaged Goods are produced by our actions and the actions of others. Understand that hurting people have a tendency to hurt other people. The church consists of people and every individual brings something with them to the gathering place of worship.

The church is not a building made of brick and mortar, but the individual and collective body of believers. The church must be representative of the kingdom of God and be ready for Jesus' return. Know this fact, Jesus is coming back again! He is coming for His bride, the church, without spot or wrinkle. Therefore, the church must know who she is and her purpose. Every person who proclaims Christianity has the responsibility for living out of the Spirit of God that dwells within. Every Christian is to produce more soldiers for the kingdom of God. This production process begins with every Christian living a Holy Ghost filled life by taking on the character of Christ and being a shining light in a world of darkness. Jesus is the light of the world. As the church, we are to light the way for others by drawing them to the body of

Christ and letting them know they are precious to God. When the church knows who she is and knows her purpose Damaged Goods are lessened.

What are Damaged Goods? Simply put, Damaged Goods are products that have been ruined, marred and cast out for destruction. Yet, still good to be used by God. We were produced by God, which makes us products of God. He produced (formed) us in His image and likeness (Genesis 1:26). We are the up close, personal intimate work of God. We are direct descendents of God because he breathed himself in us (Genesis 2:7). God took personal care for all humanity when He created us just a little lower than the angels (Psalm 8:5). The first Damaged Goods were ruined and marred in the Garden of Eden when the serpent took advantage of the innocence of Eve to bring Adam to a fall (Genesis 3:4). By taking advantage of them, the serpent damaged Adam and Eve along with their intimate relationship with God.

It is by nature that we are born in sin and iniquity. We are human and struggle with the flesh on a daily basis. As children of God, we must bring our flesh under subjection. "Those who belong to Christ Jesus have crucified the sinful nature with its passions and desires" (Galatians 5:24, NIV). This is not an easy task when we live in a world that seduces the mind to convince the flesh. It is important that we spend time walking with God daily and sitting down at the table He has prepared for us. We must allow Him to cleanse us by His anointing and fill us with an overflow of His Holy Spirit. "Thou prepares a table before me in the presences of mine enemies, thou annointest my head with oil, my cup runneth over" (Psalms 23:5).

Unfortunately, some persons who profess to be Christians take on the characteristics of the serpent and produce damaged goods instead of disciples. This is why the church is to maintain damage control in situations, behaviors that attempt to cause damage to the body of Christ, and the reputation of God's kingdom. We are to be peacemakers, "blessed are the peacemakers: for they shall be called the children of God" (Matthew 5:9). We are the children of God. It is God's desire that there be peace within the church.

Every situation may not have a resolution, but it can be managed with a loving spirit toward one another. Although one person's issue may not seem important to a large body of people, it is important to that individual. Therefore, the church must look beneath the surface to address the need. Every place Jesus went there was an issue of need to be met. Each time, no matter how big or small the issue, Jesus took time to minister to the need at hand.

It is time for the church (Christians) to stop making Damaged Goods! It is past time for making disciples as commanded by the Great Commission of Jesus Christ. We must "**Go and make disciples** of all the nations..." (Matthew 28:19, NLT).

Chapter 1

THE CHURCH

Prayer: God, please give me an understanding of the ekklesia (the church) and my responsibility as the individual church. Lead me in the way that I can be of excellent service to you and the people you place in the path of my life. Let my light so shine before men that they may see my good works and glorify you. In Jesus name I pray. Amen.

The Church

What is the church? The church is not a building. The church is not an institution. The church is not an organization. Collectively and individually, the church is a living organism filled with the Holy Spirit of God and organized by God. Thus, the living organism is every believer who is a part of the body of Christ. The church has character and is made of mind, body and soul. So, the real question is not, what is the church, but who is the church?

In the Greek translation church is defined as *Ekklesia*. Otherwise known as, the called out from the world. God has called out every believer by name. "…I have called you by name; and you are mine" (Isaiah 43:1, New Century). The church is you, me and all Christians who have been created by God for His divine purpose. We are called out as living testimonies with an assignment to fulfill the great commission. The called out from the world are to be living epistles.

> *"Ye are our epistle written in our hearts, known and read of all men. Forasmuch as ye are manifestly declared to be the epistle of Christ ministered by us, written not with ink, but with the Spirit of the living God, not in tables of stone, but in fleshy tables of the heart."* 2 Corinthians 3:2-3

As living epistles, our lives are to be reflective in the likeness of God. This was God's way of reproducing himself in humankind. "And the Lord God formed man of the dust of the ground, and breathed into his nostrils the breath of life; and man became a living soul" (Genesis 2:7). Man became a living soul called unto holiness, *"You must be holy, because I am holy"* (1 Peter 1:16, NLT). To be holy is to live out of the spirit of the living God that dwells inside of us. Just like Adam received Eve as being one with him, the church is to be one in the same spirit with Christ. Adam received Eve unto himself by saying, "This is now bone of my bones, and flesh of my flesh..." (Genesis 2:23). Through Christ, God has received every believer unto himself, "For we are members of his body, of his flesh, and of his bones" (Ephesians 5:30).

The Character of the Church

Christ came as an example for the church to take on his character, which is the purification of holiness. Christ is one with God and we are to be Christ like. "Whosoever shall confess that Jesus is the Son of God, God dwelleth in him, and he in God" (1 John 4:15).

"Clothe yourselves therefore, as God's own chosen ones (His own picked representatives), [who are] purified and holy and well beloved [by God Himself, by putting on behavior marked by] tenderhearted pity and mercy, kind feeling, a lowly opinion of yourselves, gentle ways, [and] patience

[which is tireless and long suffering, and has the power to endure whatever comes, with good temper]. Be gentle and forbearing with one another and, if one has a difference (a grievance or complaint) against another, readily pardoning each other, even as the Lord has [freely] forgiven you, so must you also [forgive]. And above all these [put on] love and enfold yourselves with the bond of perfectness [which binds everything together completely in ideal harmony]." Colossians 3:12-14, AMP

Clothing ourselves everyday by taking on the character of Christ will make a great difference in the life of the church. Walking in the path that is straight and narrow will keep us focused on living out of the Spirit of God that dwells within us. Taking on the character of Christ requires us to have love, joy, peace, longsuffering, gentleness, goodness, faith, meekness, and temperance (Galatians 5:22-23).

The Character of Christ

Love (Agape)

Love is the core character of Christ that is not condition based and have no strings attached. It is something that cannot be bought, destroyed, or left to deteriorate. Love is the substance that binds all the characteristics of Christ within the believer. Love makes it possible for the church to live out of the spirit of God that dwells within it. The church is to love beyond measure, and does not give weight to the material things of this world or keep a count of what it has done for others. The church must be open with compassion for people from every walk of life without any ulterior motives or personal gain. The real church knows how to love because God is love (1 John 4:8).

Joy

The joy of the Lord is strength that will keep the church (Nehemiah 8:10). Having Christ like joy gives the assurance of God's grace. The church must allow God's great joy to resonate in its spirit. Having joy in the church will encourage others when all seems lost. As the church, we are responsible for encouraging others and bringing them to the well of living water.

Peace

Maintaining a mind fixed and stayed on God will keep your thoughts and heart right with God. Peace is what Jesus left with us through the Holy Spirit. Having peace let us know that all is well with God and there is no room for chaos to take control of the mind. It is the peace of God which passes all understanding that keeps the mind of the church (Philippians 4:7).

Longsuffering (Patience)

The church has to have patience with others. With patience the church will endure to the end and never give up on others who are seeking relief from God. The church must run the course, but run with patience (Hebrews 12:1).

Gentleness

To be gentle is to handle with care. A gentle spirit makes a difference and does not bring harm but protect. "And the servant of the Lord must not strive; but be gentle unto all men…" (2 Timothy 2:24)

Goodness

The church must have goodness and seek to know truth and give honor. The church must be just in all things regardless of the cost. The church must show goodness to others and not turn a blind eye when a difference can be made by doing right. The goodness of God will continually endure in all situations (Psalm 52:1).

Faith

Faith is to believe and trust God in all circumstances. Know that God will come through for you in some way. Have confidence in knowing that everything is in God's order of time. "For we are made partakers of Christ, if we hold the beginning of our confidence steadfast unto the end." (Hebrews 3:14)

Meekness

Meekness does not mean weakness. This is the characteristic of having the courage to restrain yourself even when you are angry. To be meek, is to be strong and endure the trials of life while facing persecution. "And receive with meekness the engrafted word, which is able to save your souls" (James 1:21).

Temperance

"And to knowledge temperance; and to temperance patience; and to patience godliness;" (2 Peter 1:8) Temperance is to maintain self control in challenging situations.

When we do not take on Christ's character, we cannot be the righteousness of God. Being less than righteous, the church must be open to rebuke by the Holy Spirit for restoration to righteousness.

Spiritual Detoxification

Is the character of the church reflective of God or is the church consumed by carnal works? Of course, the church is not perfect and exempt from sin. "If we say that we have no sin, we deceive ourselves, and the truth is not in us" (1 John 1:8). At no time will any person be perfectly purified and holy (i.e., without fault) while clothed in the flesh. We are to repent of our sins, strive to live a godly life and help others. Daily nurturing of God's Word is a continuous purification process for mankind to have a healthy wholeness of the mind, body, and soul. So many times, the human spirit is at risk of becoming extremely polluted that a spiritual detoxification is needed.

The church must give herself to fasting and prayer for spiritual detoxification to cleanse away the natural man. The cleansing must start from the inside out and give freedom to living a Christ centered life. This requires us to renew our minds and not get trapped in the ways of the world (Romans 21:2). The temple of God has been called to be decent and in order (1 Corinthians 14:40). From the inside to the outside, the church must be fit for carrying out the mission of the kingdom. Spiritual detoxification is beneficial because it improves the overall well being of the church. Mentally, the church will have clarity and be able to clearly hear the voice of God speak. Spiritually, the church will be able to breathe with ease and function even in times of spiritual warfare. Physically, the church will be vibrant and radiant for others to see the evidence of God's awesomeness.

The Mind, Body and Spirit of the Church

The church is three dimensional, made up of mind, body and spirit and is responsible for the reproduction of disciples. It is God's desire for the church to reproduce Christ like "Goods" by thinking like Christ, showing compassion like Christ and surrendering wholly to Christ. This does not require the church to be "Super Christians" but for the church to operate outside of self and in the supernatural.

The Mind of the Church

The church must have the mind of Christ (Philippians 2:5). What are you thinking? How are you thinking? Is your thinking in line with the Word of God? Living a Christian (i.e. Christ like) life begins with the thoughts and imaginations of the mind. The life in which Christ led before mankind while he was on the earth exemplified the expectation of how every believer who is the church must be. Yes, Christ was one hundred percent human and one hundred percent deity. However, it is demonstrated throughout scripture that with God all things are possible (Mark 10:27). This includes the mindset we should have as Christians. The mind of the church consists of what we think, how we think, our emotions, and carrying out the actions of our thoughts.

Some time ago the retailers stocked the shelves with paraphernalia displaying WWJD. This was a reminder for followers of Christ to ask themselves, "What would Jesus

Do?" in their particular situations. In order to answer this question one must be in line with the Holy Spirit. This is done through prayer, fasting, reading and studying the Bible on a daily basis. When we have the mind of Christ our thought process is no longer subjected to the carnal mind, but is overridden by the Holy Spirit. We then have the mind of Christ and can understand what the Apostle Paul meant when he said, *"For who hath known the mind of the Lord, that he may instruct him? But we have the mind of Christ"* (1 Corinthians 2:16).

Having the mind of Christ is our conscientiousness that keeps us focused on the things that will give God glory and we do not seek glory for ourselves. We lose sight of this when we allow the natural man to resurrect and override our spirit. This usually takes place when situations arise that challenges our morals. It is human nature for us to have a moral war, especially when doing what is right may not seem favorable for us at the moment. Be assured that it is only for a moment and "all things work together for good to them that love God, to them who are the called [*Ekklesia*] according to his purpose (Romans 8:28). It is human nature that when we want to do good, evil is present (Romans 7:15-16). The mind of Christ is the voice of reason that resonates within us when our flesh is warring against our spirit (Romans 7:22-23). The more Christ minded we are, the easier it becomes to put the flesh under subjection to the authority of God and be at peace.

The mind of Christ keeps us at peace in the midst of whirlwinds. *"Thou wilt keep him in perfect peace, whose mind is stayed on thee; because he trusteth in thee"* (Isaiah 26:3). Keeping our mind stayed on God results in greater communion and fellowship with him. We must *"gird up the loins of our mind..."* (1 Peter 1:13), have clarity of mind for the preparation of ministry to the masses. Having the mind of Christ will prevent idle thoughts of negativity, doubt and misunderstandings when interacting with others. Too many times within the church, as a collective sub group and individually, discord is created among Christians who allow themselves to be used by the adversary. It is at this time, all imaginations of the mind must be cast down and truth will be known (2 Corinthians 10:5). The adversary will be put on notice and will have to be subjected to the authority of God. No longer will the mind of the church be taken captive by the devil.

The Body of the Church

The church is the body of Christ and was created for God's glory. Our flesh is only functional because God breathed Himself into us. Our physical bodies are the temples where the Holy Spirit dwells within every Christian. "What? Know ye not that your body is the temple of the Holy Ghost which is in you, which ye have of God, and ye are not your own? "(1 Corinthians 6:19). We must take care of our bodies by nurturing them with physical food and water. We must exercise our bodies to keep fit and limber. We are to take care of our bodies from the inside to the outside.

Just like the physical body, the body of Christ is made up of many parts. Each body part has a particular function and purpose. It is the same with the church body. Every Christian receives at least one spiritual gift from the Holy Spirit. These gifts are not for our keeping, but for us to share with others for building the kingdom of God. "He [Holy Spirit] hand out gifts of apostle, prophet, evangelist, and pastor-teacher to train Christ's followers in skilled servant work, working within Christ's body, the church, until we're all moving rhythmically and easily with each other,…" (Ephesians 4:11-13, Message). The whole body suffers when one function of the body is not in rhythm. God created the church to be balanced like the physical body. Do our hands and arms compete against each other? No, they work together for the purpose of accomplishing a goal.

Too many times, the church has operated like the world by being competitive and taking on worldly ways. Too many times the lifestyle and character of the church has contradicted the will of God by being self righteous and pushing people away from the fellowship. Paul had to admonish the Church of Corinth because they became competitive. Competition is not of God! Holy Spirit administered the various gifts for the edification of the church and for God to receive the glory. "There are different kinds of spiritual gifts, but the same Spirit is the source of them all.

There are different kinds of service, but we serve the same Lord. God works in different ways, but it is the same God who does the work in all of us. A spiritual gift is given to each of us so we can help each other" (1 Corinthians 12:4-7, NLT).

Church, time is drawing near for us to meet God face to face. The gifts we received from the Holy Spirit must be used for the edification of the people. We are to let our lights so shine (Matthew 5:16) that others will be drawn to the kingdom. As the body of Christ, we are to desire the ultimate perfect will of God for others and ourselves. The ultimate perfect will of God is that no one should perish, but have eternal life (John 3:17).

The Spirit of the Church

The spirit of the church has been connected with God from the beginning of humankind; the breath (spirit) of God gave life to Adam (Genesis 2:7). Living out of the Spirit of God will always be accompanied by instructions for God to receive the glory. The Spirit of the church should be a spirit with a zest and zeal to preach the gospel and set the captives free (Isaiah 61:1; Luke 4:18). The Spirit of the

church is beyond our conscientiousness of prophesying,

dreaming dreams and seeing visions (Joel 3:28). There will

be signs and wonders as evidence of God's Spirit in the

church. The spirit of the church bears witness to who we are

in Christ. "The Spirit itself beareth witness with our spirit, that

we are the children of God: And if children, then heirs, heirs

of God, and joint-heirs with Christ…" (Romans 8:16-17).

When we, as the church, have finished our earthly

assignment, our spirit will return to God (Ecclesiastes 12:7).

What Kind Of Church Are You?

There is a song that asks the question, "What kind of

church is this?" The response, "This is a hand clapping,

tongue talking, sanctified church." The clapping hands is to

praise God, the tongue talking is to be holy edification giving

sanctification to the body of Christ. This is not always the

case. Sometimes the church goes through the motions just

because it is the ritual. God is not pleased with ritual praise

because it is in opposition of giving Him glory and edifying the people.

When God spoke to the Apostle John he gave him a vision with a message concerning the seven churches. The Lord's message to every church was, "He that hath an ear, let him hear what the Spirit saith unto the churches" (Revelation 2:7, 11, 17, 29; 3:6, 13, 22). Each church was given commendations and/or rebuke regarding their actions as a collective body. The commendations were for their good works, patience, spiritual perseverance, faith, and diligence in keeping sound doctrine. The rebuke was for their loss of love, tolerating worldliness, disobedience, and spiritual conceit. These same commendations and rebukes holds true for the church [us] today. We must listen to the voice of the Lord and be obedient to the mandated call God has placed upon our lives. Each church represents the character of individuals and groups within the church family today. After all, we are the church and God is still speaking to us today. The church must live out of the spirit of God that dwells within and examine itself daily. "Examine yourselves; whether ye be in the faith..." (2 Corinthians 13:5). Let's look

at the messages to the seven churches and examine
ourselves as the church.

The Ephesus Church

The Ephesus Church was commended for being full of
zeal to do good deeds and service. They willingly gave
unselfishly to the community and other causes in the name
of the Lord. The Ephesus Church labored for the kingdom,
demonstrated patience and refused evil doers and liars.
They would not tolerate anything that would be an offense to
God. This included the false teachings that the Nicolaitans
tried to bring into the church. The Nicolaitans taught that
continuing in the same sin is okay when followed by
repentance. Sin in any shape, form or fashion is not okay.
This is so contradictory of God's word and does not honor
Him. "He that committed sin is of the devil; for the devil sins
from the beginning…" (1 John3:8). When willful sin,
including false doctrine, takes place it is not of God's will.
One may argue, as justification, that all have sinned and
fallen short of the glory of God (Romans 3:23). However, to

knowingly continue in sin, especially the same sin, is not of God. When regeneration has taken place, conviction and correction will rule in the life of the church. "No one born (begotten) of God [deliberately, knowingly, and habitually] practices sin, for God's nature abides in him [his principle of life, the divine sperm, remains permanent within him]; and he cannot practice sinning because he is born (begotten) of God" (1 John 3:9, AMP).

Although the Ephesus Church continued to be steadfast with a faith in God, they were rebuked for neglecting to maintain a heart for God (Revelation 2:4). They became more diligent with service to the community, family and other "busy work" that they steered away from truly worshiping God. Some churches today are still doing "busy work" on the Sabbath by giving more attention to functions for social organizations, participation in sports, shopping and other things that take the place of worship.

The Smyrna Church

The Smyrna Church was commended for their

missionary work and enduring persecution. The Smyrna Church was impoverished and rich at the same time. They were impoverished by the standards of the world but spiritually rich with a kingdom inheritance. They gave up all their worldly riches to follow Christ. The Smyrna Church trusted and believed God for their well being and totally surrendered their lives for the cause of Christ. They welcomed persecution and would be considered martyrs. Much like the apostles, the Smyrna Church counted it worthy to suffer for the sake of Christ. "...they had called the apostles and beaten them...and they (the apostles) departed...rejoicing that they were counted worthy to suffer shame for his name" (Acts 5:40-41).

There was no rebuke for the Smyrna Church. They may have been the church "without spot or wrinkle" after all the persecution they endured. Apparently, the Smyrna Church stood their ground and did not allow worldliness in any form to pollute or bring them toxins. Are there churches/individuals today willing to go through persecution and give up all worldly goods (i.e. homes, jobs, investments, etc...) to do mission work in the field locally and abroad?

The Pergamos Church

The Pergamos Church was commended for being steadfast and faithful despite the evil corrupt environment that surrounded them. They remained active in winning souls for the kingdom, but allowed idolatry and corrupt doctrine in the church. This was due to much of the support for the church coming from the government. The Pergamos Church was rebuked for tolerating the corrupt doctrine of Balaam and allowing those who were not true believers to participate in the church. This is considered to be sacrilege on the part of the unconverted. How much do the church/individuals allow the government to be involved in the administration of the church practices? For example, receiving government funds to assist with meeting the needs and/or desires of the community can limit how the church can minister to the community about the love of Jesus.

The Thyatira Church

The Thyatira Church was commended for their charity, spiritual service, faith and patience. They remained faithful to God when their leaders were more interested in being a part of the elitist in the world. The Thyatira Church refused to allow the backslidden state of others to discourage them from their walk of faith.

The Thyatira Church was rebuked because of their lax in discipline. They were tolerant of an occult prophetess, Sambathe. She is referred to as a "Jezebel" (Revelation 2:20).[1] Sambathe was so corrupt that she seduced the people of Thyatira and convinced many of them to mix idolatry and sexual impurity with their Christianity. She was controlling and filled their minds with false doctrine. As a result of the Thyatira Church being lax, the leaders of the church strayed away from the Word of God and broke intimacy with God. An example of this kind of church today would be a church/individual who exploits the gift of God for personal gain. How about those money lines for healing? Does this line up with the Word of God? Simon, the

---

[1] This information was extracted from the book, Christ and His Seven Churches What the Messages to the Seven Churches of Revelation Mean to Us Today, C.A. DeLatte, Published by Fairmont Books, 1999 (pg. 12, 75)

sorcerer, offered money attempting to purchase the gift of the Holy Ghost. The apostle Peter told Simon that the gift of the Holy Ghost cannot be purchased with money (Acts 8:18-20).

The Sardis Church

The Sardis Church had no commendations for the majority of their members. A small group of members were commended for faithfulness and their works. Those who were faithful were commended for their purity and devotion to Christ. However, their works were not perfect before God.

The Sardis Church was rebuked for being spiritually dead. They were in a backslidden state not giving their lives to Christ. The Sardis Church did not live the life that was in line with the Word of God. Simply put, this is the type of church today where there is no evidence of authentic ministry; the church/individual is worldly with no spiritual morality.

The Philadelphia Church

The Philadelphia Church was commended for their faithfulness, keeping Christ's Word and not denying him.

They resisted the evilness of others and refused to conform to the ways of the world. The Philadelphia church continued to persevere in their loyalty to Christ and the truth of the gospel. There was no rebuke and the Philadelphia Church was without "spot or wrinkle." Today's model church of Philadelphia would be the church/individual willing to uphold the gospel truth, serve the community without the motive to gain recognition of self, and have a heaviness of heart for souls to be saved.

The Laodicea Church

The Laodicea Church received no commendations. They were recognized for having works, but the works were not pleasing to God. It appears that the works may have been evil. The Laodicea Church had a spiritual condition of being lukewarm. The Laodicea Church accepted compromise with the world. They looked very much like society; with one foot in the church and one foot in the world. This is the church/individual that seeks popularity and desires to be accepted by society

Self Reflections, Thoughts and Questions to Ponder

Do you consider yourself to be the church? Why or why not?
What are you doing to maintain your character with God's
expectation of you?
When was the last time you examined the mind, body and
soul of your church as a collective body?
When was the last time you did a personal examination of
your mind, body and soul?
What kind of church are you?

Chapter 2

DAMAGED GOODS

Prayer: Most gracious and kind Father, give all of your people the mindset to have a heart to live out of the love of Christ and be obedient to your will. Lord, for every damaged good I look for you to take inventory and make brand new. In Jesus name I pray. Amen.

Sometimes others will unintentionally cause damage because of self preservation. When in fact, it may be the opposite of what they encountered in the past. There are occasions when the church (collectively and as individuals) may not know they have damaged another brother/sister in the body or someone who may be searching for God.

An evangelist asked an individual who appeared to no longer be in fellowship, "Do you attend church? Why or why not?" The individual responded, "You have no right to judge me! I know what you are trying to do—I will hurt you before you hurt me. All of you 'church people' are the same!" At that moment, the evangelist realized the individual had been damaged by the church and attempted to reassure the individual that there was no judgment being placed on him/her. Depending upon the answer of the individual, the evangelist had no motive other than to invite the individual to church or at least fellowship outside the four walls. The individual never answered the question, but the evangelist prayed with the individual and left an open invitation for fellowship.

Looking at the world and taking inventory of some "Damaged Goods" (the people of God) there has been a great attack on their lives to try to make them give up, throw in the towel and even walk away from God. Several of these individuals willingly shared their "Damaged Goods" experiences as a testimony to their faith and their advice to others.[2] Many of the experiences that these "Damaged

---

[2] All names have been changed and stories are written as they were told.

Goods" encountered were with "the church" (individually and collectively). These individuals are not claiming to be victims. They are just telling their stories about how they had been damaged. This is not about being a victim, but how they dealt with being damaged by others in the body of Christ. These stories should not be looked upon as insignificant or measured against our own personal standards. Some of these individuals walked away from the church as a whole, but not from God. Others stayed with the church and grew deeper in their faith.

Interviews

Favoritism is not of God and should not be a practice of the church. "My dear brothers and sisters, as believers in our glorious Lord Jesus Christ, never think some people are more important than others" (James 2:1, NCV). It is unfortunate that this particular practice of the world is practiced when the body of Christ comes together.

Suzy

Suzy was looking for a church home hoping that she

would be able to find a place of acceptance. Suzy came from a family where her father was of the Greek Orthodox Church, and her mother was of the Serbian Orthodox Church. Suzy's upbringing was in the Greek Orthodox Church. Suzy shared that as a little girl she came into the true knowledge of Christ by her grandmother. Her grandmother would share Christian literature with her. When Suzy was about eight years old she understood that Jesus Christ died and saved her from her sins. Her grandmother then told her that she was a Christian. Suzy recalled becoming very upset and telling her grandmother, "I am not a Christian! I am Greek Orthodox!" Suzy said she was hurt until she understood the difference between a denomination and salvation. During Suzy's high school years she felt that she was treated differently by other Christians (i.e., her teachers) because she was not allowed to have her Christmas days in January instead of December.[3] When Suzy became an adult she moved away from her hometown to another city where there was only one Greek Orthodox

---

[3] The Greek Orthodox Church celebrates Christmas in January.

Church. At this church, Suzy was unwelcomed and snubbed

by the members of the congregation on her first visit. She

believed this behavior towards her was because she did not

appear to have money. (In reality, Suzy came from a well to

do family.) This became evident when Suzy returned to the

church with a relative who had money, status in society, and

is a member of the congregation. The congregants then

realized who she was and wanted to treat her better. Suzy

wanted no connection to these people and never returned to

the church.

After Suzy's mother passed she had another

encounter of what she described as being damaged by "the

church." Suzy's mother requested that her body be donated

to an institution for research upon her death. The institution

cremated her mother's body after the completed study. At

the same time, Suzy desired to have closure with a memorial

service at the Serbian Orthodox Church.[4] The church

refused to allow a memorial service because Suzy's mother

was cremated. This was damaging to Suzy because she

---

[4] The Serbian Orthodox Church does not believe in cremation.

believed it insulted her mother's numerous years of dedication and service to the church.

Suzy stated that her whole experience with some professed Christians, "the church, in the realm of society, has been that many of the leaders and frequent church attendees are bias, cheaters, and thieves." Needless to say, because of her experiences she no longer attends church and has no plans on returning to church. Suzy says that she is a Christian (not perfect), she prays, and she talks with others who have a serious walk with God.

Suzy advises: "Keep looking to God, pray and just believe."

There are many people who do not realize that others outside of the church body are watching them daily. Outsiders are watching the way proclaimed Christians present themselves on the job, in social settings, and other public places. Sometimes people who do not profess to be Christians seem to know more about the expected behavior of a Christian. No matter what, all Christians should walk the talk by living according to the Word of God; "Always be humble and gentle. Be patient with each other, making allowances for each other's faults because of your love" (Ephesians 4:2, NLT).

Jefferson

Jefferson is a gentleman who has professed Christ as his personal savior. He holds fast to his beliefs and his security of eternal life. Jefferson could not really say he had any experience of being misused, mistreated or hurt by the church. However, during his work experience he met people who seemed to have strong religious beliefs and believes that "Whoever claims to live in him must live as Jesus did" (1 John 2:6, NIV).

Jefferson encountered persons in authority who professed to be Christians but their lives demonstrated otherwise. For instance, some of them were womanizers and excessive drinkers. Their conduct was not in line with what the Bible instructs for Christian living. Jefferson said he worked for a "well to do" individual who professed to be a believer but at the same time believed that "he who controls the gold makes the rules." The individual did not display the Christian behavior that he claimed. This was hurtful for Jefferson to see Christ misrepresented. Jefferson does not claim to be the perfect Christian. However, he believes that people who profess to have strong Christian beliefs should have control of their actions and strive to live a holy life daily. Biblical teachings and training should help Christians to take their walk with God to heart.

Jefferson advises: "Everyone should hold on to their faith and understand that life happens and things will get better."

There are occasions when we encounter people who fit the "holier than thou" category. They may mean well and believe they are doing everything that God has commissioned them to do. They are so self-righteous that they do not realize how much they have fallen short of the glory of God. Because of their self-righteousness others may reject fellowshipping with other believers, have doubt about their own relationship with Christ, or never give their life to Christ. "For I say unto you, that except your righteousness shall exceed the righteousness of the scribes and Pharisees,

ye shall in no case enter into the kingdom of heaven"
(Matthew 5:20).

Shelley

Shelley remembered that as a child the church
(congregation) took care of each other. Shelley has
experienced church as the congregation of like believers
expressing themselves by corporately worshiping God
together. Shelley said that all who profess Christ and believe
is to be representative of the church. For her, being in the
service of worship is a moment of solidarity and peace from
the world.

Shelley said her father-in-law (actually her husband's
stepfather) was a minister who lacked piety and was a male
chauvinist. Her mother-in-law was the church gossip. In
Shelley's eyes, her in-laws did not demonstrate a Christian
life as leaders in the church.

Shelley said she began doubting God because of
what she witnessed happening in the lives of other
Christians and their reactions to the situations. Shelley gave
as an example that a friend of hers (she believed was a

Christian) lost her sister to cancer and blasphemed God. Later, Shelley became aware that her sister, who loved God tremendously, had been molested when they were younger. She noticed the change in her sister's behavior. Shelley said she had an aunt that was a devout Christian. Her aunt was married with two children. Her aunt's husband was not saved and cheated on her aunt numerous times. Shelley watched her aunt diminish as she turned to drugs and away from God because of her living situation. Shelley could not understand why a loving God would allow these things to happen to people who trusted Him. Especially to her sister and aunt who were very active in the church, knew the Word and had a great love for God. After this, Shelley did not attend church on a regular basis.

Recently, Shelley heard one of her co-workers praying and inquired about his church. He told her the name of his church and invited her to the fellowship. Shelley accepted the invitation and began attending morning worship on a regular basis. Shelley became a member of this congregation and was excited about having a new church home. She was assigned a "big sister" to help her continue in her faith walk. This was short lived because her "big sister" did not keep in touch with her. Nevertheless, Shelley did not give up because she wanted to have a solid connection with her new church home. As means to do this she began to attend church school. Sadly, her church school experience was not successful. Shelley felt that she was overlooked and not welcomed into the class. Shelley did develop a decent relationship with her pastor and loved his spirit. However, the pastor seemed to be a hustler. The pastor would ask for extra offerings without giving an explanation and promote his side business for the congregation to join his ventures. It seemed like he was more interested in making money than the spiritual well-being of the congregation. Currently, Shelley attends church but not on a regular basis. She understands that there is no perfect church and is currently seeking a church home. Shelley says she was very trusting of people until a friend told her, "Closed eyes are not always shut."

Shelley advises: "Still hold on to your faith in God.

Regardless of the hurt and pains you may endure. Find a church home that believes in taking care of their people. Read your Bible. Keep the faith."

It is important to know God for yourself and trust what His word is personally saying to you. The Word of God is of one interpretation and many applications. When someone misinterprets the Word of God, we must approach the person with love and compassion to help give understanding. Philip, the apostle, demonstrated this when he shared the scriptures with the Ethiopian. "And Philip ran thither to him, and heard him read the prophet Esaias, and said, understandest thou what thou readest? And he said, How can I, except some man should guide me? And he desired Philip that he would come up and sit with him" (Acts 8:30-31). We are not to make others feel inadequate because of our extensive knowledge. This can be intimidating and hurtful causing a person to disconnect from the fellowship. "Yes," said Jesus, "what sorrow also awaits you experts in religious law! For you crush people with unbearable religious demands, and you never lift a finger to ease the burden." (Luke 11:40, NLT)

Phillip

Phillip says that those who believe and have a relationship with God are the church. He believes that he is faithful in his own personal walk with God. Phillip attended church in his youth and lives by the Word of God as he understands. Phillip believes the church is supposed to operate differently from the world, yet church politics remain. He believes the politics of the church is parallel to the politics of government, and just about everyone (in the church) wants power and control.

Phillip has been turned off by the political ambitions and dictatorship of the church. It is his opinion that many pastors have a dictatorship mentality like the government. They use their position in leadership as means to exercise power over the people they lead. Phillip believes this because some pastors he has associated with seem to believe that they are the only ones with whom God communicates; and they know everything because of their academic achievements in theology. Phillip was told (by one pastor) that his understanding of the Bible is wrong. Phillip does not believe a pastor should tell an individual that their interpretation of how God spoke to them through the Bible is incorrect. He commends them for the knowledge they have acquired from their formal education in theology; however, people should be able to read and take from the Bible what they believe God has placed in their heart. Phillip believes that when a pastor denies a person their belief of how God has spoken to them can be hurtful and discouraging to their faith.

Phillip says that he does not purposely seek to introduce others to having a relationship with Christ. He has no expectations for others in the body of Christ and ignores their behavior. He does not allow the behavior of others to effect the expectations he has for himself. His expectations are to "Strive to do his best in living right before God. Keep it moving and not say anything to others." Phillip said that when he has observed people being unjust toward others he can only shake his head and believe that God will work in the situation. Phillip does not attend church because of the power play and the "mini cults" within the church. Although he does not attend church, he is willing to fellowship with others outside the four walls.

Phillip advises: "Listen to the person and talk them through. Tell them to do the best they can do. Encourage them to keep the faith and walk first in their own personal relationship with Christ."

Pride has no place in the body of Christ. The fellowship of believers should be a safe haven. Many times pride gets in the way of meeting the needs of others who come into the fellowship. In many cases, a person comes to the fellowship because they need a hug, wisdom, godly counsel, and acceptance. However, these needs are overlooked because of the "unholy agendas" and competition within the church. Too many individuals do ministry as means to promote themselves to greatness while demeaning others within the congregation. "These six things doth the LORD hate: yea, seven are an abomination unto him: A proud look, a lying tongue, and hands that shed innocent blood," (Proverbs 6:16-17)

Victoria

Victoria joined fellowship with a new church and had to deal with others in the church that are "cliquish with an unholy agenda." This group of people was unwelcoming and did not like new people coming into "their church" with new ideas. Some of the things Victoria described are how the older women envied the younger women, leaders who have held positions for years are prideful and do not treat people right. Victoria noticed that a number of persons in leadership positions are not willing to serve with their whole heart. They refuse to do the "grunt work" of ministry by going into the trenches. Not having a heart hinders the ministry from moving in the full force to reach the masses.

In addition, Victoria has observed the attitude that others within the body of Christ have toward the pastor's wife. It is a hurt to her heart when the pastor and his wife are not given respect as leaders in the church. Victoria recalled a time when some of the church members wanted to do something nice for the pastor and his wife; but they were told by the "selfish leaders" that it was not appropriate. Victoria says that she has received backlash from some of the same leaders in her church when she is fulfilling her ministry duties, as directed by the pastor. Nevertheless, she continues to serve them because of the love she has for God. Victoria knows that if she did not know God or have the love of God she would probably be in jail because of the treatment she has received from other Christians.

Victoria advises: "Know yourself and the reason you attend church. Go fellowship with like believers and have an expectation of a word from God. Focus on your personal relationship with God. Have a strong prayer life and let God speak to your spirit and heart. Those who are in leadership need to be obedient and minister to others as God orders. Be sure to minister with the love of God."

Bobby

Bobby believes every individual who has accepted Christ is "the church" and should serve as an ambassador of the church as a body. Many church leaders have not shown themselves to be of great service as an ambassador. Bobby and his family united with a church several years ago. After one of the services he decided to purchase an audio recording of the sermon. Instead of receiving a copy of the sermon, Bobby received an audio recording of a meeting between the deacons and some of the elders of the church. These same deacons and elders did not care for the pastor, but they maintained his leadership because of his prominence in society. The pastor had no knowledge of this particular meeting. On the recording, Bobby and his wife heard these church leaders having a negative discussion about his family and another family that belonged to the congregation. Based on the conversation the deacons and elders were devising ways to have the families removed from the church or at least make them leave. They were not happy with the thought of having these families, who were new to the congregation, bringing in new flourishing ministries. This group of leaders desired to destroy their ministries. After Bobby listened to the conversations he confronted the leaders about the recording. One of the

deacons denied being a part of the meeting although his

voice was heard. This same deacon later apologized and

asked Bobby to provide him a copy of the recording. Bobby

kindly informed him that he would need to purchase his own

copy from the media ministry. Bobby also shared the

recording with the pastor. The pastor immediately addressed

the situation from the pulpit. At that time, other families

within the church began to clap and whisper among

themselves that it was about time the actions of these

leaders were brought to the forefront. After this, other

families and individuals within the church came forward

about the things these particular leaders had done to them

and others. This was a definite indication that these leaders

not only caused damage to the families they were

discussing; but they damaged an entire congregation of

approximately 425 people. The entire church was damaged

and there was division in the body due to a combination of

issues that were not discussed. Bobby's family and many

others left and went to another church, some people stayed

and some left without officially joining another body of believers.

Bobby also mentioned being invited to the home of deacon "Joe" (a firefighter) and his wife, "Karen" (a warehouse worker) when his family first joined this congregation. Bobby said he and his wife looked at this as an opportunity to fellowship with another couple in the sense of ministry. Needless to say, Joe and Karen were seeking another couple for sexual exchanges of spouses. They were swingers! Bobby and his wife steered clear from this couple. Then there was another female deacon who wanted to sleep with Bobby. She had a reputation throughout the church of making it her "mission" to sleep with other people's husbands. Bobby said that one of the elders was found to be a thief and had no problem stealing from his secular job. All of these leaders mentioned were seasoned leaders in this congregation prior to the current pastor coming to the church. The more the current pastor tried to make correction with the leadership, the more they rebelled.

Bobby and his family united with another church after

his job relocated to another city. Here, the pastor attempted to transition the leadership by creating new leadership classes. This was because in times past, deacons were being elevated to elder positions even though they continued to be rebellious. People were competing for positions in the church for self elevation (i.e. deacons and elders) and most of them were not qualified for the positions they were seeking. To Bobby, this seemed to be the world working itself into the church. Bobby's observation is that many people have walked away from the church because they have been hurt. However, they did not walk away from God. Bobby said a friend of his shared with him that he loves God and is in fellowship with a church, but he has not established membership due to his church experiences.

Bobby and his family left these churches without any regret. Bobby said these church experiences made him get closer to God. He and his family moved their membership to another church and are actively involved in ministry.

Bobby advises: "As a newcomer to a congregation a person should seek relationship from others in the congregation that is grounded in the spirit of God. This is for the purpose of extended fellowship outside the four walls of the church. Know God for yourself. This way you can lead others to Christ by being an example to others."

Jaxon

Jaxon's story began when he was about 13 years old. Jaxon hails from a lineage of pastors and he was very observant of his grandfather's ministry. Throughout the years, Jaxon heard numerous stories about how his grandfather made personal sacrifices to help his congregants and others throughout the community pay rent, buy groceries, and get some of them out of jail. Yet, some of these same individuals mistreated his grandfather and this was hurtful to Jaxon's heart. It was hard for Jaxon to understand why people would act in such a way.

In the mid 1980's, Jaxon's grandfather had to deal with power struggles within the church. He recalled two individuals on the trustee board who challenged his grandfather's duties as chief leader and wanted to change the church into an organization. This caused a great deal of confusion and hurt to the entire church body and the community at large because the church was then split. This had an even greater impact on Jaxon's family because the trustees stole his grandfather's retirement. Jaxon mentioned that these trustees were benefactors of sitting at their dinner table with his grandfather as youth. Jaxon viewed them as being Judases toward his grandfather. Looking through the eyes of a teenager, Jaxon shifted his view on the church, especially trustees who did not have the pastor's best interest at heart.

Despite the hurt Jaxon encountered by witnessing the actions of the church toward his grandfather, he accepted his call to ministry and has pastored for over 20 years. Jaxon stated that he had trust issues with trustees because of what his grandfather had to endure. Jaxon recalled a situation when the trustee board became upset about the purchase of meat for an anniversary dinner. The trustees argued that the purchase should not have taken place without their knowledge. This took joy away from the ministry for him.

(Yes, Jaxon had a flashback of trustees at his grandfather's church.)

Jaxon also mentioned a more personal hurt he had with the church. This was a painful hurt of gossip about his son. Jaxon's son was dealing with some issues and gossip about his son spread throughout the church and the community.

Jaxon advises: "In spite of the church hurt we've endured, we still have to understand God still speaks to the church (collectively). If we are not in that place (forsaking the assembly) we can miss God, we can miss our destiny, and we will not be complete. You cannot be complete without being in His [God's] house."

Kaytie

After being a member in the pew for three years Kaytie decided to join the hospitality committee. Kaytie has a heart for people and believed that she could be used by God to welcome people. She chose the hospitality committee because the team seemed to be very warm and welcoming. On the contrary, the hospitality committee turned out to be wolves in sheep clothing. Once she became a part of the committee it seemed to be a double standard. They were to work as a team but at the same time they were not. Some of the group congregated among themselves as a clique and were not inclusive or welcoming to others who joined the ministry. Other people who joined the hospitality ministry at the same time as Kaytie also felt excluded. This is known because she noticed they dropped out of the ministry immediately, and Kaytie inquired about the reason they were no longer a part of the hospitality ministry. During meetings, the hospitality committee was informed of two things: (1) they were not to hold conversations with each other when they are on their post, and (2) if they are late they are to take the posts that are not covered. However, there were many of them who still held conversations and insisted on having a specific post. Kaytie recalled an incident where one of the ladies, who had been in the ministry for a long length of time, arrived late and was not happy when she seen Kaytie on what she believed was "her post." As a result, the ministry lead assistant moved Kaytie to another post and place the lady on the post she wanted. Kaytie became angry and thought about the incident while sitting in church. This shifted her focused from the worship service. She then decided to quit the hospitality ministry. After quitting, none of the members on the committee contacted her to see why she was missing from the ministry. They had all of her contact information (e-mail, address, phone number). Almost a year later, after she quit, she received an e-mail from the ministry inviting her to a bridal shower. The e-mail said, "If you want a husband come to the shower. Bring a gift if you want to be blessed with a husband." Kaytie did not know a gift was contingent upon God blessing her with a husband. Furthermore, these individuals still had not inquired about why she was not visible in the ministry. This rekindled Kaytie's anger and made her want to send an unholy response to the e-mail. She did not address the issue because she was already frustrated and did not want it to turn into something confrontational. She did not tell her pastor or the associate ministers about her experience because she believed they were too busy. Since this experience Kaytie has not been active in any ministry. However, she is exploring other possible ministries. Although she was hurt by the actions of the hospitality committee it did not deter her from going to church to receive the word of God and fellowship. The experience made Kaytie continue in her walk with Christ and increase her prayer life. Kaytie understands that we are all on different levels of maturity in the body. She believes that there are those in leadership that should not be in leadership. Maybe these leaders are not cognizant of what they are doing or no one has addressed the issue.

Kaytie advises: "Do not give up! We have to think about why we come to church and that we do not come for the people. Know that we are coming to church to get our strength from God. Keep coming to church. Don't let other people's actions discourage you from coming back to church."

Ayalah

Ayalah did not grow up attending church on a regular

basis. As a child, she knew church as the place that would feed her and her siblings breakfast on Sunday. This is no longer the case for her because she has come a long way. Ayalah accepted Christ when she became an adult and is now an elder at her church.

Ayalah shared that her first experience with church hurt was when her son had graduated from high school and was not celebrated by the youth ministry. Her son was also hurt by this. He was the only senior at the church this particular year. Her son was denied the opportunity to apply for a scholarship from the church. Although he was the only individual graduating from high school at the church he should have been given the same treatment as others who graduated in the past. The church did not have a dinner in his honor as they had done in the past or other graduating seniors. He did not receive any gifts from the church upon his graduation like the church body has done in the past, as prior to them becoming members of the church. At one time Ayalah was the director over the youth ministry. During her time as director, she and her son surrendered whole-heartedly to the ministry. It was very hurtful to her that the ministry she had led in the past had taken such a dramatic turn in how, when and whom they would recognize upon their graduation from high school. When a dinner was given for her son none of the team from the youth department attended. The only persons in attendance was Ayalah, her son and the pastor. Her son was not given any financial support from the youth ministry to assist him with college.[5] Ayalah said that she had a heated discussion (accompanied by unholy language) with her pastor about how she felt. She was very angry and frustrated with Robin, the director of the youth department, whom she believed was at the core of all the confusion. Ayalah said God prepared her not to expect anything from the church body as a whole. Other individuals from the church gave her money to assist her son with his first year of college. Robin told Ayalah that the church will not be contributing toward her son's education because of

---

[5] Every year the youth ministry would give a financial gift to the graduating seniors.

the monetary gifts she personally received from individual members. Because of her maturity and obedience, she shielded her son from experiencing a lot of hurt from the church. Ayalah envisioned that upon her son's graduation from college, she would "hold up fingers to the house (the church)" and she would leave this church. This was a statement that she wanted to make. Ayalah was convicted by the Holy Spirit because the way she wanted to handle the situation was not in line with God's word. She was thankful that there was room for correction. She and her pastor had a conversation that helped her overcome this battle. The conversation resulted in a greater understanding and level of respect that she lacked. This was not helpful to her son. Ayalah began to realize that as a leader, she had to remove herself from being "mom" to being "priest." With this being the case, Ayala could not allow her son to hate the church and walk away because of this situation. There was a period of time that she did not speak to Robin. Ayalah admitted that she was tempted to have a few words of exchange with Robin, but God did not let that happen. As a matter of fact,

Ayalah's healing process began when Robin contacted her and made a request for her to teach a lesson in her absence. It just so happened that the lesson to be taught was about dealing with hurt. After teaching the class, Ayalah met with Robin, hugged her and told her they were done. Ayalah said the Holy Spirit increased her maturity in the situation because against her own will she began speaking to Robin. This subsequently resulted in Robin surrendering herself to the spirit of God in Ayalah, and their relationship started to mend. Ayalah made a conscience decision that she would make sure no other young person would have to have the same or similar experience as her son. It is only by God's grace that Ayalah remained at her church.

Ayalah advises: "Ask yourself, 'why do you go to church? Is it for man or is it for God?' If it is for God, you have to be confident that God is going to give you victory over the situation. If you are going to church because it is church, rededicate your life to Christ so that you can grow up in God, not in church."

Sierra

Sierra accepted Christ at an early age and has remained steady in her faith. Sierra is a preacher and comes from a long line of preachers, teachers, singers and evangelist. Sierrra says that it is by the grace of God she has not lost her mind because of some church experiences. Sierra's story has a combination of being hurt within the four walls of the church and being hurt by the church outside the four walls. Sierra stated that she was a member of the evangelism team at her church. The evangelism leader, Minister Johnson, yelled at her in front of the evangelism team for no legitimate reason. The other team members were taken by surprise and did not understand why Minister Johnson would do such a thing to her. At this moment, Sierra wanted to walk out of the room and never return. However, other members of the team were encouraging to Sierra and she remained on the team.

Sierra believed that those who have the name of Christ (i.e. calls him/herself Christian) must demonstrate who they are 24/7. This means in the fellowship of believers, at home, social events and anywhere. Sierra shared her experience about "Madeline," a co-worker, who professed Christianity. Sierra stated that Madeline was not very nice to her unless she wanted something. Sierra recalled Madeline sending her mean e-mails and causing discord in the office. Yet, Madeline would seek biblical advice from Sierra on how to handle certain situations with her personal relationships. This angered Sierra because the very person that was trying to destroy her career had the nerve to ask her for spiritual advice. She had to seriously pray for Madeline and herself. It is because of prayer and her walk with God that Sierra did not choke the life out of Madeline. Sierra repented for her ungodly thoughts about Madeline.

Sierra advises: "Stay strong in the Lord, in your faith. Do not allow anyone else to hinder your walk with God or staying in church. Continue to serve others with the servant heart of Jesus Christ. Consult God on every issue in your life, especially when it comes to the church."

Crystal

Crystal is a person who loves God, married and has two sons. Crystal went to her pastor for counseling on an issue she had concerning her husband's refusal to attend church. Crystal said that during the counseling sessions, the pastor gave her advice and asked if she could possibly persuade her husband to come into the office for counseling sessions. Her husband did not believe counseling sessions were necessary because he had no interest in attending church. After several counseling sessions, the pastor made a pass at Crystal and touched her inappropriately. Crystal was devastated that her pastor would violate her. This was a person she trusted to help her, not hurt her. Crystal said she was raped in her early twenties, and the actions of her pastor resonated memories that she tried to forget. She could not understand why her pastor would try to take advantage of her. Crystal said that she did not tell her husband what happened. Since the incident, she has not attended church on a regular basis. Crystal still believes there are some good pastors out there who have a true heart for the people.

Crystal advises: "Keep on loving God, believing God and getting to know God. Don't let anybody or anything stop you from having a relationship with God. Know that everyone has some kind of issue, including the pastors."

Self Reflections, Thoughts and Questions to Ponder

How have you been hurt by the church? If so, how did you react?
Has the actions of others stopped you from serving in a ministry or going to church?
What would you have done differently in the stories presented? Why?

CHAPTER 3

LEADERSHIP MAINTANENCE

Prayer: God forgive me if I have caused damage in the lives of other people. God help me that I will live peaceably with all men. In Jesus name I pray. Amen.

Damage Accountability

In the previous chapter, those who shared their stories all had one obvious thing in common, they were hurt by leaders in the church. This is awfully sad because the leaders are those who are responsible for guiding, encouraging and uplifting others. Understand that being a leader in the church is not limited to the pastor, elder, teacher, deacon, minister of music or someone who is influential within a congregation. Every person in the congregation is a leader because people follow the examples of others.

It is a great burden for a leader to be responsible for others and have to be accountable to God. The prophet Ezekiel was called to be the spiritual watchman. He was responsible for looking after the souls of Israel and held accountable to God for any neglect of his duty.

> *"When a righteous man doth turn from his righteousness, and commit iniquity, and I lay a stumblingblock before him, he shall die; because thou hast not given him warning, he shall die in his sin, and his righteousness which he hath done shall not be remembered; but his blood will I require at thine hand." (Ezekiel 3:20)*

Ezekiel was not necessarily comfortable with having the responsibility, but he had to be obedient to the call of God. This responsibility required him to give warning to those who turn away from God. Some leaders may be uncomfortable with the responsibility of giving warning to others, but when leaders fail to lead with accountability they cause others to fall out of righteousness. The body of Christ is responsible for bringing souls to salvation and being our brothers/sisters keeper. The actions of leaders towards others in the body of Christ and abroad may be the very thing to turn others away from the fellowship. Thus, their blood will be required at the hand of the leaders. An example of this would be a leader who is set on the following standard set by man.

The standard: "All persons who desire to be in the choir must audition."

Supporting Scripture: There is no scripture found to support this standard.

God can use anyone he chooses. Man's least likely is God's most likely. Leaders must realize that God calls whom he qualifies, not whom man qualifies. Moses had a speech impediment, but God qualified him to lead Israel out of Egypt (Exodus 3:10). David was a shepherd boy, but God qualified him to be king over Israel (1 Samuel 18:7, 12). The nameless woman at the well was an outcast, but God qualified her to be an evangelist. She left her water pot and beckoned others in the city, "Come see a man, which told me all things that ever I did: is not this the Christ?" (John 4:29)

Leaders are to lead by the Word of God so that souls will be saved. Leaders are called to be someone others can look to for building up and not tearing down. Many times we have heard people (in and out of the Church) comment, "If that person is a Christian, I don't want to be one." It is ashamed to hear this statement when time is drawing near for the return of Christ. Today is a critical time for church leaders to have urgency for bringing lost souls to Christ. Too many souls are hanging in the rafters and wandering to and fro. Leaders need to follow the leading of the woman at the well by inviting others to Christ.

Damage Control

Many Christian leaders are pushing people away from Christ. Jesus told the scribes and Pharisees how hypocritical they were because of how they prevented others from having the opportunity to enter into the kingdom of heaven. He gave warning to them for being false leaders, putting on a facade of being holy on the outside and having a corrupt heart.

"Woe unto you, scribes and Pharisees, hypocrites! For ye are like unto whited sepulchers, which indeed appear beautiful outward, but are within full of dead men's bones, and of all uncleanness. Even so yea also outwardly appear righteous unto men, but within ye are full of hypocrisy and iniquity" (Matthew 23:27-28).

Corrupt thinking leads to corrupt behavior. Wherever there is corruption you will find behaviors of hypocrisy, lying, abuse of authority, wrongful use of position, and competition. Crystal's story (Chapter 2) would be an example of a leader using his position to take advantage of another person. The world breeds corruption and people will do whatever it takes to obtain a title and/or have a position of authority. The Word of God tells us not to be conformed to the world and to think differently from the world (Romans 12:2). Too many times the ways of the world are brought into the church (usually by leaders) causing damage to the body of Christ.

Managing Conflict in the Church

Conflict is inevitable and is a part of human nature. *"If it be possible, as much as lieth in you, live peaceably with all men."* (Romans 12:18). We will never be able to control conflict, but we can resolve or manage it. "All things are possible with God" (Matthew 19:26). Let's take a moment to review some of the ways conflict was managed in the early church among the leaders.

Conflict begins with an individual's thought and/or action toward another person. Many times people make assumptions based on what they perceive to be true. It is at this precise moment, that their imaginations lead them to believe false information. The false information breeds fear, competition, jealousy, envy and division. This is all based on perception, not discernment that is given by the Holy Spirit. It is important to differentiate between perception and discernment. That which is perceived in the mind is not always the truth. The church must guard the mind daily by putting on the helmet of salvation (Ephesians 6:17). The church must not give thought to things that are not of God by "Casting down imaginations, and every high thing that exalteth itself against the knowledge of God, and bringing into captivity every thought to the obedience of Christ" (2 Corinthians 10:5). Discernment is given by the Holy Spirit and brings forth truth.

Pastors are often responsible for resolving and/or managing conflict in the body of Christ. There are times when the pastor will delegate this task to other leaders. This is what Moses did by the advice of his father in law, Jethro (Exodus 18:13-23). It is unfortunate that a great deal of the conflict in the church is caused by the leadership. When Paul spoke with the Corinthian Church regarding the divisions among them, he took responsibility as a leader and managed the conflict. One example can be found in 1 Corinthians 11:18-24. In order to manage or resolve the conflict, Paul had to identify the issue, listen, observe, and focus.

Identify the issue.
--There is an elephant in the room sucking up the oxygen. Yes, the people of Corinth saw the elephant of division. Paul recognized and identified the issue.

> "I hear that ***there be divisions*** among you, and I partly believe it."

(1 Corinthians 11:18)

Listen.
--Listen to those who feel they cannot breathe because the elephant has taken up space. The people of Corinth became frustrated because nothing was being done about the elephant. They continued to complain because they wanted to breathe.

> "For there must be **heresies among you**..." (1 Corinthians 11:18)

Observe.
--Be watchful and pray with a discerning spirit that the issue will manifest itself. In addition to listening, Paul observed and seen the elephant revealed itself.

> "For ...they may be **made manifest** among you" (1 Corinthians 11:19)

Focus.
--Keep the focus on the cross. Maintain a Christ centered atmosphere. Paul knew that the elephant was huge. Therefore, he reminded the people of Corinth not to focus on the elephant. He reminded them to remember Christ as the focus.

"When ye come together therefore into one place, this is not to eat the Lord's Supper." (1 Corinthians 11:20) "…this do in remembrance of me." (1Corinthians 11:24)

The issue was not the elephant itself but the actions of the elephant. The issue probably was not resolved, but it was managed to the best of Paul's ability. The church has a variety of issues that may not have an absolute resolution. However, conflict can be easily resolved when individuals know and accept their place in the church. This is what took place when dissention occurred between the Greeks and the Hebrews in the book of Acts.

> *"And in those days, when the number of the disciples was multiplied, there arose a murmuring of the Grecians against the Hebrews, because their widows were neglected in the daily ministration. Wherefore, brethren, look ye out among you seven men of honest report, full of the Holy Ghost and wisdom, whom we may appoint over this business. And the saying pleased the whole multitude…" (Acts 6:1, 3, 5)*

In short, this conflict had many variables but not difficult to resolve. The disciples identified the issue, listened, observed and focused on means for a resolution.

As leaders, they brought two conflicting parties together and had both parties select from among themselves who would be able to make a final decision for handling the daily distribution. The disciples actually set them up for arbitration. Nevertheless, the matter was resolved because it "pleased the whole multitude."

Unfortunately, much of the hurt and damage is not addressed by the pastor or the appointed leader. Therefore, causing further damage and distrust within the church. The pastor and/or other appointed leaders must determine the best way to manage the issues/matters that are brought before the church.

Self Reflections, Thoughts and Questions to Ponder

Do you believe it is important to resolve and/or manage issue/matters in the church?
How would you have addressed the elephant in the room?
If an issue/matter is of a great concern to you, would you bring it to the attention of the leadership? If not, why?
Do you trust your church leaders? If not, why?
Have you taken inventory of how you lead others in ministry? Think about how you can make a positive impact in leadership.

CHAPTER 4

LOOKING BENEATH THE SURFACE

Prayer: Father God, please help me to see others as you see them. Use me God to touch the hearts and souls of your people that I can give agape love and look beyond their faults, pain, shame, and see their need. Help us to love beyond measure. In the name of Jesus I ask it all. Amen.

Many times in this life we fail to see the emotional, physical, mental and spiritual abuse that others have suffered. This is because we have our own agenda and forget about having compassion for others. We often think about the hurt we have encountered and the negative things others have done to us. It is our duty as the church to have compassion and pay close attention to the needs of the people. Jesus gave us an example of how to have compassion on the people.

> "I have compassion on the multitude, because
> they have now been with me three days, and
> have nothing to eat: And if I send them away
> fasting to their own houses, they will faint by
> the way: for divers of them came from far"
> (Mark 8:2-3).

When Jesus showed compassion to the multitude he had seen their emotional, physical, mental and spiritual needs. The multitude had an emotional need to be with Jesus. The spiritual need was also being met as they witnessed the many miracles Jesus performed. For three days they journeyed with Jesus, and he knew that none of them had eaten. Jesus then made provision to meet their physical need. If the multitude was sent away without the nourishment of food, they probably would have lacked mentally (clarity of mind). Jesus looked beneath the surface. *Where did the hurt come from?*

People encounter hurt from many different social settings; such as, family, work, and other social organizations. There are some people who will say they have never been hurt by the church. Yet, they will admit to being hurt in other social settings by family members, friends, coworkers and other people. You may be wondering how this is related to being hurt by the church. Usually, there is at least one Christian represented in each of these settings. As stated in chapter 1, every Christian individually is the church.

Family is our first point of social life from birth. In the Christian family there is an expectation that everything that is said or done is to be pleasing to God. Unfortunately, there are situations that take place within the Christian family that does not please God. We know the story about the spouse who attends church regularly and consistently use ungodly language but desires his/her spouse to give their life to Christ. The spouse to whom the language is directed has been hurt by the church. We know the story about the parents who attend church and abuse their children. The children have been hurt by the church. We know the story about the Christian relatives or close family friends who have cheated, stolen and violated other family members. The family members have been hurt by the church.

Friends and coworkers are the second point of social life. How is it possible that a person can be hurt by the church in school and/or the workplace? School and the workplace is where we meet the world outside of our family structure. The world encourages adaptation to the ways of society. Some Christians have adapted to some of these ways and have caused damage to others. For example, a supervisor (a Christian) knew one particular subordinate (a Christian) was the center of chaos in the office. The supervisor held the other subordinates at fault for the chaos caused by their coworker. The other individuals were hurt by the church. Another example is when a coworker (a Christian) has damaged the reputation of another coworker. This coworker whose reputation was damaged had been hurt by the church. These are just a few examples of real life situations that are overlooked or shrugged off as being petty. What may be petty to one person is not petty to another and should be taken in consideration.

So, why are people being hurt by the church? The

answer to this question is simple, hurting people hurt other people. Although this is believed to be a true statement, it does not mean that it is always the intent of hurting people to hurt other people. As previously demonstrated, people are hurt in various places in their lives by the church.

Baggage Claim/Check

Hurt is baggage on the inside of us that has been claimed but not always checked. Therefore, the claimed baggage is carried from place to place, including the place of worship. Everyone has an open invitation to come as they are to the house of worship. Those who accept the invitation come with the expectation that they will be accepted no matter what condition they may be in at the time. When they arrive, they bring their claimed baggage full and heavy from the hurt, nicks and wounds of life.

The baggage need to be checked. Although the baggage is heavy, they refuse to check it, empty it, and be relieved of the excess weight of the world. The baggage has to be checked to discard the contents that are making it heavy. The baggage is to be given to the Lord. "Casting all your care upon him, for he careth for you" (1 Peter 5:7).

Self Reflections, Thoughts and Questions to Ponder

Do you demonstrate the love of God to your family?
Do you have a lifestyle of worship at all times?
Have you offended others intentionally or unintentionally?
Do you show genuine compassion to others?
Do you treat others in a way that is pleasing to God?
Where did your damage come from?
Do you have some baggage that need to be checked?

Chapter 5

NO MORE DAMAGE-BE HEALED

Prayer: Dear God, you said that anything that I ask in your name according to your will shall be done. It is in Jesus that I abide knowing that He abides in me. Your Word says, "Death and life are in the power of the tongue." My tongue is available to you, God, to speak healing where damage has been. Lord, please heal in the places where I have caused damage to the church, and heal me where I have been damaged by the church. It is in the name of Jesus I petition this prayer. Amen.

Truthfully, damage is done intentionally and unintentionally. Either way, damage has been done and healing must take place. The spoken words and physical actions of others cannot be undone. It is like trying to take back the ringing of a bell when you already heard it or unscrambling an egg after it has been cooked. So, how do you heal damage after it has been done? Finding the answer begins with prayer and the willingness to forgive those who have caused damage. All of us have caused damaged and has been damaged.

Prayer

We must pray continuously with perseverance, effectiveness, fervency and in confidence. "Pray without ceasing" (I Thessalonians 5:17). We must be "Praying always… in the Spirit, with all perseverance and supplication for all saints" (Ephesians 6:18). Staying in continuous prayer guarantees a closer relationship with God, and we begin to be more like Him. We become more aware of how we are treating others and how to handle the way we have been treated.

Prayer establishes our dependency on God. It keeps our mind intact us as we go through this journey of life. There are times that it seems like the damage increases the more we pray, while we pray, and after we pray. This is when we might feel as if God has deserted us or he no longer has an interest in hearing our pleas and supplications.

Church, this is far from the truth because God cares about all of us. Praying with sincerity, confidence and believing God's word brings us closer to our healing. We are to pray in confidence for healing. "And we are confident that he hears us whenever we ask for anything that pleases him" (I John 5:14, NLT).

Spiritual, mental and physical healing

Being damaged can be taxing on an individual spiritually, mentally and physically. Many times we become damaged in the face of adversity, and we must continue to pray. We must pray with a heart of faith and expectancy knowing that God will deliver. There are times when it may seem difficult to pray for ourselves. This is when the Spirit intercedes on our behalf (Romans 8:26). We have the blessed assurance of knowing that communicating with Jesus throughout the day makes everything alright.

The woman caught in adultery was spiritually damaged. It is quite evident that while she was facing her accusers she had a prayer of hope in her heart for deliverance from the damage to her reputation. Surely, her spirit was low as she experienced public persecution preparing to be stoned to death. The people damaged her by making her a public spectacle and causing her to have a foul reputation. In the end, she was still standing delivered from her accusers. Jesus inquired, "Where are those thine accusers?" The woman replied, "No, man, Lord." (John 8:9-11). She had just a little talk with Jesus that made it right.

No matter who we are our reputations should be important to us as the church. There have been times when words or actions of one person can be damaging to the church as a whole. Has anyone ever asked you about your place of worship? Keep in mind, you are the church. The way you present yourself is a reflection on your place of worship. With this being the case, it is important to stay prayerful that what we say and/or do may not be damaging to others. Sometimes the church can be like the crowd of accusers ready to throw stones in judgment. By doing this, the church will hurt itself and damage its own reputation. Pray for the spirit of the church to be healed.

The church/individuals can become mentally

damaged when the Word of God is not demonstrated in lives of the people. The mental damage seems to occur in the place of worship when someone (who has a Jezebel spirit) is intimidated by another person's gift and views them as competition. The Jezebel spirit is controlling and attempts to sabotage another person's ministry, while at the same time seeking opportunity for self elevation.

Elijah was mentally damaged. Because of Elijah's work Jezebel sought to destroy him so that she could reign. Elijah became mentally damaged the moment he surrendered a portion of his mind to Jezebel when he received her threats to destroy him. Mental anguish had taken over his thought processes because he allowed fear to enter into his mind. He prayed for God to take his life because of what he had to face as one being pursued for execution by Jezebel. "But he himself went a day's journey into the wilderness, and came and sat down under a juniper tree: and he requested for himself that he might die; and said, It is enough; now, O LORD, take away my life; ...." (1 Kings 19:4). God responded to Elijah to let him know that he will escape the sword (1 Kings 19:13-17). Elijah had a little talk with the Lord and everything was made right.

There are Jezebel spirits that will take the mind of the church if there is a lack of prayer. The Jezebel spirit will take assault on the mind and come against God at every turn. When Jezebel spirits are encountered it affects the mind and people will sometimes take flight from their place of worship. We think straight by keeping our mind stayed on the Lord (Isaiah 26:3). We must not run but be bold for the kingdom (Proverbs 28:1). We must not allow fear to be an option because God has not given us a spirit of fear (2 Timothy 1:7). Pray against the Jezebel spirit for the church to be free from mental damage. "Greater is he that is in you than he that is in the world" (1 John 4:4).

Being damaged spiritually and mentally has an effect on the physical health of the church. When the church is spiritually and mentally damaged, the body becomes disjointed and the tendons deteriorate. When one part of the body suffers the whole body suffers.

Jesus Christ was physically damaged. "He was

wounded for our transgressions and bruised for our iniquity"
(Isaiah 53:5). He prayed to the Father that, if it were
possible, the hour might pass from him. And he said, "Abba,
Father, all things are possible unto thee; take away this cup
from me; nevertheless not what I will, but what thou wilt"
(Mark 14:35-36). While Jesus was earnestly praying, His
body was in physical agony and his sweat was as drops of
blood (Luke 22:44). Although he prayed, He knew that he
had to be the sacrifice for the sins of the world. Because of
His physical damage, the church no longer has to be
disjointed. Jesus is the tendon that holds the
church/individuals together spiritually, mentally and
physically.

Church, we are to pray for the physical body to be
healed. When one part of the body rejoice, the whole body
rejoices (1 Corinthians 12:26). Each person is important and
can be used for the glory of God. There must be balance in
the body of Christ. That balance begins with the church
uplifting one another.

Pray for one another that spiritual healing will

manifest. Heal from the inside to the outside. Heal the mind, body and spirit of the church. Pray for others, desire to be filled with knowledge, wisdom and understanding. "For this cause we also, since the day we heard it, do not cease to pray for you, and to desire that ye might be filled with the knowledge of his will in all wisdom and spiritual understanding…(Colossians 1:9)."

God is sovereign and answers prayer the way he chooses that is in accordance to his will for our lives. Therefore, we are to pray for God to increase in us that we will decrease (John 3:30). We are to pray daily for understanding, wisdom, knowledge and discernment. This will result in understanding God's will for our lives; a daily dose of wisdom will help us decide how to handle hurt; and knowledge coupled with discernment will aid us in recognizing malicious spirits with the intent to hurt versus innocent spirits with no intent to hurt.

Forgive

To be healed, we must make forgiveness a habit. This

is a good habit because forgiveness is healing. "He forgives all my sins and heals all my diseases" (Psalm 103:3, NLT). Forgive ourselves and others on a daily basis. There are those times when we hold onto baggage and refuse to check it. When we surrender our baggage to God it is easy to forgive those who have hurt us. Peter asked, "How many times must I forgive?" The Lord answered, "Seventy times seven. If he sins against you seven times in one day and says that he is sorry each time, forgive him" (Luke 17:4, NCV).

Some of us have heard the saying, "forgive and forget." Forgiveness does not always come easy. As for forgetting, that is even more difficult depending upon the severity of the hurt. Some things are to be remembered as life lessons. Jesus said, "And forgive us our debts as we forgive our debtors" (Matthew 6:12). The life lesson, only lend what you can afford to give away.

Reconcile

When we reconcile with each other God is pleased

and his glory is shown through us. It is God's desire for the church to live in harmony. We are to be able to come together and resolve our differences. "Forbearing one another, and forgiving one another, if any man have a quarrel against any; even as Christ forgave you, so also do ye" (Colossians 3:13). God is relational. It is his will for the church to also be relational and value one another. This is why he sent Jesus to keep us in right relationship with him. God reconciled us to him by Jesus Christ, and has charged us to reconcile with one another. "And all things are of God, who hath reconciled us to himself by Jesus Christ, and hath given us the ministry of reconciliation" (2 Corinthians 5:18).

God has uniquely made each of us for his pleasure and glory. There are times when God is not pleased with our actions and/ or words. Yet, he forgives us and keeps us in relationship with him. We are to do the same with one another. When we are offended by another person, we are responsible for letting them know about the offense immediately. Do not let the sun go down on your wrath (Ephesians 4:26). Holding on to anger is not healthy. God wants us to be in good health.

With His stripes we are healed!

The church is healed as individuals and as a collective body of Christ. There is a difference in being healed and being cured. To heal is to give newness and all the corruption and blemishes are gone and exists no more. (E.g. the healed lepers, Marian of leprosy, the woman with the issue of blood, the blind man from birth) When there is a cure, the symptoms may go away, but the residue of the disease will remain. There are no biblical references indicating that Jesus cured. There is no account of any person returning to Jesus with the same ailment. As the church we are to heal the wounded with pure agape (love) having a heart for God and his people. Right now, declare and decree "with his stripes we are healed" (Isaiah 53:5). NO MORE DAMAGED GOODS!

Self Reflections, Thoughts and Questions to Ponder

Are you praying your way through the hurt?
Have you forgiven those who hurt you?
Have you attempted to reconcile with those who have hurt you?
Are you harboring years of anger?
Do you consistently reflect on things that happened many years ago? If so, ask yourself why?
Do you want to be free of the hurt? If so, pray and ask God to remove the anger from you. The hurt will be gone immediately if you sincerely give it to God.
Tell yourself out loud every day, "I am healed of my wounds! I am not giving up on my faith! I surrender myself whole being to God.

CONCLUSION AND FINAL THOUGHTS

All of us have been damaged goods.

All of us have caused damaged to others (intentionally or unintentionally).

Being damaged by the church can have several affects:

- It may cause discord throughout a congregation.

- It can damage the reputation of the church body

- It can impact an individual's decision to not fellowship with any church

- It can make a person second guess the true missions of the church

- It can contribute to a person's decision to turn away from God

This is just to name a few. Nevertheless, it is the responsibility of the church to be aware of its character, actions and reactions to situations.

I AGAPE YOU! BE BLESSED MY BROTHERS AND SISTERS!

ABOUT THE AUTHOR

Elder Treneé L. Pruitt is a native of Dayton, Ohio. She was raised with Christian values and teachings with the understanding of "…as for me and my house we will serve the Lord." (Joshua 24:15) Elder Pruitt confessed Christ as her personal savior at an early age and began her Christian service at Tabernacle Baptist Church in Dayton, Ohio in many ministries.

In 1991, Elder Pruitt relocated to Toledo, Ohio. She united with Friendship Baptist Church under the leadership of her father in the ministry, Bishop Duane C. Tisdale. She served in the choir, was the assistant Youth Coordinator/Advisor/teacher, and the evangelism ministries.

Elder Pruitt currently belongs to Oakley Full Gospel Baptist Church in Columbus, Ohio under the leadership of Overseer Jonathan J.H. McReynolds. She was ordained as an elder on February 20, 2004, by Bishop Andy C. Lewter, Jr., predecessor to Overseer McReynolds. She is the Evangelism Coordinator for the Oakley Full Gospel Baptist Church and District Director of Evangelism for Full Gospel Baptist Fellowship International Columbus. Additionally, Elder Pruitt has been divinely assigned for extended ministerial service at Second Baptist Church, New London, Ohio under the pastorate of Jamie R. Richardson.

In early 2005, Elder Treneé L. Pruitt founded Healing Hearts Beyond the Walls to reach out to the spiritually wounded. The mission of Healing Hearts Beyond the Walls is to restore health and heal wounds. "I will give you back your health and heal your wounds says the Lord…" (Jeremiah 30:17). Elder Pruitt preaches, teaches, motivates, encourages and empower others as a part of her laboring for the Kingdom of God. In addition, she is a public speaker, entrepreneur and above all things sold out to God.

Elder Pruitt earned a Master's in Public Administration, a Bachelor in Theological Studies; and a Bachelor in Business Management.

For speaking and/or teaching engagements contact Elder Pruitt at the following e-mail address: **Healingheartsbtw@gmail.com**

www.ingramcontent.com/pod-product-compliance
Lightning Source LLC
Chambersburg PA
CBHW062005040426
42447CB00010B/1924